CREATIVE CURRENT

50 ideation techniques to spark your lightbulb

AKSHAY DINAKAR

CREATIVITY

is not a trait unique to a few lucky individuals who are born with an ability to effortlessly come up with clever team names, construct the tallest marshmallow-toothpick tower, and wow others with their ingeniously simple, yet profound solutions that make you grumble, "Why didn't I think of that?"

The truth about creativity is that it's a lot like leadership. Sure, we can agree that some people start out with a slight genetic edge in their ability -- but with the right mindset, strategies, and thought tools, anyone can nurture both qualities to the point of excellence.

This book equips you with a starter pack of 50 out-of-the-box, creativity-catalyzing ideation strategies that will ensure that you'll never struggle with sparking your lightbulb again.

This is your **CREATIVE CURRENT**.

01

FORCED MORPHOLOGY

Choose an object that is completely unrelated to the product you are designing, and "borrow" relevant features from that object that you can integrate into your final product. Force morph a water bottle and a ziploc bag? Camelbak.

02

DOODLETHINK

Snag a blank sheet of paper and a pen, choose an abstract word (like "motion" or "history") and ferociously doodle for 3-5 minutes with the goal of filling the page with an interpretative composition inspired by your word of choice. Turn on some eclectic music in the background as you doodle-think! Once you're done doodling, stand a few feet back from your drawing and identify a holistic meaning from your impromptu masterpiece.

03

RANDOM PAGE INSPIRATION

Grab the largest novel you can find off the nearest bookshelf, and flip it open to any page. Read that page, paying as much attention to detail as if it were the final clue to a hidden treasure. Once you finish scrutinizing the text, brainstorm solutions that could improve the situation that the novel's characters are facing, enhance the setting of the novel, or solve the book's conflict, fully acknowledging that you've only read one page of this novel. Despite this lack of context, these kinds of "snippet solutions" can be surprisingly profound!

04

BEYOND THE LYRICS

Look up the lyrics to one of your favorite singer's lesser known songs. While reading the lyrics, envision the story or scene that the musical artist is trying to describe. Identify any conflicts present in it that could be solved with a creative solution.

05

ALEATORICISM

Aleatoricism can be thought of as the integration of "chance" or "randomness" into the process of creation. Go to a public location (perhaps a local library), find a computer, and open up its browser history. Pick a random number between 1 and 20, and then count that many links down in the browser history. Check out whatever web-page that takes you to (assuming it's not too weird or sketchy!), and you might stumble upon some inspiration.

06

SENSORY OVERLOAD

The adrenaline rush that comes with vibrant sensory stimulation can sometimes catalyze the flow of all sort of interesting ideas. You can place yourself into a sensory over-whelming environment by visiting one, or by constructing the setting yourself. Visit a crowded urban setting near you with lots of people and action (think environments like NYC's Times Square or San Francisco's Fisherman's Wharf), or create artificial stimulation by staying in your room, blasting music while flashing holiday lights, and feasting on sugar candy or popcorn... it's up to you!

07

TOP DOWN DESIGN

An effective problem solving technique, top down design (also referred to as holistic thinking) is a way of zooming out from the situation and identifying the underlying problem and its solution, rather than getting caught up in the details. Metaphorically imagining that the conflict you're dealing with is a giant, complicated machine -- top down thinking is all about figuring out where the machine's primary "on switch" is, and if the power cord is plugged into the wall.

08

BOTTOM UP BUILDING

The inverse of top-down design, bottom up building (also referred to as analytical or relational thinking), is a way of zooming into the situation and focusing on the individual details/relationships between parts of the problem in order to tweak one component and achieve a solution. If we return to envisioning the conflict as a metaphorical machine, bottom up building will help you find which specific gear is malfunctioning and crashing the entire system.

09

EDISON NAPPING

The time of day with the most potential for creative thought is the 10 - 15 minutes before you fall asleep, when your mind is drifting between dreams and consciousness, and the neurons in your brain are random-ly firing. Thomas Edison was very aware of this, and was known to sit in a chair with a pen and pad in one hand and a metal ball in the other. When he fell asleep, his hand would relax and the ball would fall onto a metal tray, jolting him awake with a loud 'CLANG.' He'd then quickly sketch down some ideas that had occurred to him while falling asleep on the pad, and pick the ball back up for another cycle. ZZZ....CLANG!

10

EXTREME CASE PERSPECTIVE

When designing something, it's important to consider how your extreme users might interact with your product. By putting on the shoes of both your ideal and least likely users, you can identify the weaknesses in your design and come up with creative solutions to improve your product.

11

BIOMIMICRY

Nature has an organic and unparalleled creativity. Take a walk in the woods, look up pictures of lesser known animals, or just enjoy photos of gorgeous natural landscapes on Google Images. Be sure to note the patterns in both the micro and macro scales of all things outdoors, such as the intricate symmetry of a spider web or the sediment layers of a canyon. Stealing inspiration from the Earth's environment is the first step towards coming up with ideas that are 'out of this world.'

12

LINKED WORDS

There's no such thing as a perfect synonym. Each word has its own micro-nuances of meaning. We can use this to our advantage -- try to describe whatever product you're designing in words, and look up synonyms for all of the adjectives you used to characterize your product. Consider the connotations of those synonyms, and you'll be able to come up with other creative features that you can then integrate into your original product.

13

WISHFUL THINKING

Make a wish. Imagine you had unlimited money, time, and no constraints. You can first think of an idealistic solution to a real-world problem, and then it'll be easier to ground your proposed solution to be compatible with what is actually possible, considering the capabilities of the real world.

14

BLUEPRINTING

Sometimes it can help to give your thought process a little direction. Look up the blueprint of a famous building (say the Louvre in Paris) or pick a random spot in your favorite city. Using the blueprint or streetmap as a mind-map that has already been created for you, follow the hallways or streets and try to come up with accordingly related ideas that seem to flow and connect with the same proximity and/or distance that the various rooms and streets of the blueprints/maps do. This will help organize your thought process and give a structured flow to your creativity.

15

SWAPPING UTENSILS

We often experience higher states of creative productivity when we change our normal routine or practices. If you're trying to brainstorm with a pencil + paper (or maybe a whiteboard + marker), put down those writing utensils and swap them with something else -- let's say kitchen utensils, crayons, chalk, sticks + stones, or rubber bands. See if you can come up with a creative way to log your thoughts using these uncommonly used utensils instead -- at the very least, you now know what has been inside your cabinet shelves!

16

RECYCLE TRASH

We throw away so many ideas because they don't fit into a specific "mold" that we wanted. Just because they weren't the right solution for one problem doesn't mean that they can't be the perfect solution for another! Take two ideas from a past brainstorming/ideation session that you rejected, and see if you can combine those two "trash ideas" into something of worth.

17

ADD CONSTRAINTS

Though it seems counterintuitive, a fantastic way to generate some of the most creative ideas is to add more constraints to your brainstorming process. Imagine that you're designing a car. You already have some base constraints -- you have to design a vehicle that reliably, efficiently, and safely transports humans from point A to B. Now let's add some arbitrary constraints and see how it creates a pathway for more creativity: 1) You only have $500 to build this car. 2) Every passenger must be able to fully stretch out their legs. 3) The vehicle must also be able to travel upside down.

18

IDENTITY FLIP FLOP

Adopt a different persona. Imagine yourself in a different career, socio-economic status, or cultural context, and be aware of how adopting these different perspectives influences your brainstorming process and the way you develop solutions. For whatever product or concept you were originally designing, redesign it as if you are that alter-ego persona.

19

SCALE UP SHRINK DOWN

Put on your creative Mad Hat, and let's steal a golden idea from Alice in Wonderland. Whatever product you're designing -- scale it up or shrink it down by a large size factor (say 1000x), and consider how changing the scope of your design alters the way the product operates, fulfills a unexpected need, or perhaps more efficiently solves the problem. This design exercise might reveal a slight modification you can make that will make your invention even more successful.

20

CONFLICT CONVERSATION

A diversity of opinions and the blending of different backgrounds engenders a high creative potential. If you only surround yourself with people who agree with you and share the same values, you'll never be exposed to new opinions and ideas. Get into an argument or an educated debate, and be willing to consider the alternate perspective -- you'll expand your cultural horizon and approach design with a more expansive mindset.

21

COMPETITOR PERSPECTIVE

For whatever product you're currently designing, place yourself in the future and imagine what kinds of product features your competitors might develop to out-market your product. Be cognizant of those features, and consider integrating them into your design to eliminate that business opportunity from your future competition.

22

THEMED THINKING

Choose an array of related entities (colors/shapes/etc.), and iterate through each one, ideating something that reflects the specific quality of that entity. Let's say you are designing a furniture item, and have chosen 'materials' as your array of choice. For each different material that you choose, reflect on how the material properties alters/enhances the product you're designing. This will allow you to quickly generate a wide range of adaptable solutions that are related, but have fundamentally different features.

23

FEATURE LINKING

A piggybacking brainstorming technique, feature linking is a method of quickly generating several distinct, but related solutions to a prompt. Here's how it works: for each solution you think of, choose one feature from it that the next solution must incorporate. Keep recycling this methodology to rapidly ideate feature-linked solutions until you find a great one!

24

ABSTRACT SHAPING

Draw 30 empty circles (each circle about the size of a ping pong ball) and modify each of the cirlces (add/subtract lines and doodles) to create a meaningful drawing of an object or entity, without too much thought. Try to come up with creative drawings that others wouldn't think of. Once you've done so, reflect on these different circle deviations and see if you can combine them into a related scene or solution.

25

CONNECT THE STARS

The night sky can provide inspiration and hope in other ways than just shooting stars. Go outside on a clear night with a erasable marker and a sheet of plastic/ glass and literally play connect the dots with the stars. Create a bunch of your own constellations, and then take them inside and analyze what your connected dots mean -- turn them into characters, products, and animals that have identity and stories.

26

INSPIRATION THROW

Have you ever reached a mental block while sitting by a window or open door? Chuck your pencil out of it as far as you can throw. Now go find it. While you're finding it, pay close attention to the stimuli of the surroundings, and try to exist in a state of heightened awareness. Absorb the environment, and who knows, you might stumble on some much-needed inspiration!

27

EUREKA

"Eureka" is perhaps the most famous word of inspiration. Pull a Shakespeare and invent some of your own words that feel inspirational to you. Then run around yelling them. Flap your arms, burn some calories, and then come back to your desk feeling refreshed and ready to do some brainstorming!

28

SENSORY DEPRIVATION

Sometimes you just need to empty your mind in order to think clearly -- the same reason why many people meditate. Find or create an environment devoid of any distracting stimuli. Go stand in a closet or stand directly in front of a plain wall, and try to blank your brain completely. It's okay if various thoughts flash across your head every few seconds, but try to achieve a level of calmness. You'll soon be fully recharged and ready to churn out some great ideas!

29

MANUAL TASKING

The most creative ideas often come when we are super bored. Choose an absolutely mundane task that you've been putting off for forever (such as shredding papers, putting away dishes, or raking the leaves outside), and while you're doing it set your mind free. Try to think about two broad approaches: 1) What really fun things do you wish you could do instead of what you're doing right now, and how can you steal qualities/features from those things to make your task mimic your fun things?
2) Can you ideate a solution that would make your manual task more efficient or engaging?

30

GOOD MEME HUNTING

Memes are creative goldmines. They are so funny and eye-catching because they masterfully connect two unrelated ideas using a socially recognizable character or metaphor, and they often highlight the irony of many problems in society that are yet to be solved. Go enjoy yourself some memes, and keep an eye out for the problems or issues that the memes highlight that could spur creative solutions.

31

RESOURCE REEVALUATION

Imagine that you are now in the future or have just won the lottery. Or perhaps a spaceship dropped you off on a different planet and all you have with you is one box of food + a few survival supplies. Now that you have a different set of resources, how do your end product or design requirements change?

32

REFLECTIVE REFLECTIONS

Do you have a prototype of your product, but feel like you've hit a roadblock? It might help to look at your design from a different angle and do some healthy reflection on your design methodology. With your design in hand, stand in front of a mirror and rotate your product around, considering its physical form. Engaging in this spatial analysis can help you come up with a breakthrough idea.

33

DREAM HOUSE

It's time to design your dream house. Maybe it's a Hawaiian retreat, a Martha's Vineyard hideaway, or a Manhattan penthouse. What technology, materials, layout, and features do you want your home to have? By visualizing your ideal future home, you will not only come up with creative ideas for features of your house, but you'll simultanously identify which design values are unique to you, as there are few things more personal than designing your home.

34

ASSUMPTION SMASHING

If you've already made a prototype of a design, this is a great technique to test whether you've fully explored the creative potential of your product. Examine your prototype and strongly consider what assumptions you made when designing it. Did you assume the user had access to electricity? Did you assume that the product should be a certain size? We often put unnecessary limitations on ourselves while designing without even realizing it.

35

SHADOW WATCHING

There's something amazing about the way we can construct meaning out of blurry/non-specific stimuli. Shadows (especially moving shadows from a bonfire, flickering light, or setting sun) can serve as great creativity catalyzing stimuli. Sit down in a spot, relax your mind, and find a hazy shadow to psychoanalyze. As it moves, give it a name, a form, a story. See if you can convert it into the shape of a product, a character, or a setting.

36

INSPIRATION EAVESDROPPING

When you go outside, take your earbuds out of your ears. You can listen to music later. Otherwise, you're missing out on an entire sense that can bless you with all sorts of creative simuli. Don't be creepy, but always be aware of what conversations, sounds, and interactions are going on around you. Go to a coffee shop or train station and people watch. Start conversations with strangers and absorb everything.

37

CHARACTER DESIGN

You've just been hired by an animation studio to design the main character for their next big hit movie. Who will it be? What will the character look like? If a caricature or simplified representation of this character were made, what features of the persona or personality would definitely be included? What makes this character likeable or unforgettable? What story does the character have to tell? What products would this character need in their life?

38

ANIMAL WATCHING

Animals are amazing sources of creative inspiration. Animals move spontaneously, and are masters at finding the most evolutionarily straightforward way to achieve an objective. Go for a walk in the woods, find a secluded courtyard, or visit your local zoo. Spectate a scene for an extended period of time and see what you can learn or ideate based on the objective that the animals seem to want to accomplish, and the means by which they are doing so.

MOVIE SCENE IMPLANTATION

You've just been cast as an extra in a blockbuster movie. As you watch the stars do their stunts and grow familiar with the plot, you can't help but wish the spotlight was on you. What invention of yours could alter the plot enough to thrust you into center stage?

40

ENHANCED STILL LIFE SKETCHING

Place a bunch of random objects a few feet in front of you (such as a bowl of fruit, household appliances, clothes) and draw them, still-life style. While you're drawing these unrelated objects, try to connect all of them in your drawing and turn them into some sort of composite object. Let your art skills and imagination do the inventing for you!

41

SUPERHERO SKILLSET

Choose a superhero power that you wish you could have, and ideate an invention that would allow you to replicate that "superhero skill." If you feel this invention is too idealistic, scale it down until you have something that is realistic and practical.

42

ALPHABET
ARRAYS

Perhaps my favorite road trip game is a simple one in which players take turns naming elements of a set (such as countries or animals) -- with the catch being that each successive element has to start with the letter that the previous element ends with. Play this game with yourself, using "product features" as the type of element, and you'll soon have a creative and diverse list of attributes you can integrate into a useful invention.

43

STARTUP SMASHUP

Choose five completely unrelated celebrities (for example, Lebron James, Khloe Kardashian, Neil Armstrong, Jimmy Fallon, and Ed Sheeran) and imagine that they have all been placed in a startup bootcamp, tasked with founding their own business venture. What product would these celebrities create together?

44

SPATIAL INTERACTION

Every artist or "creator" knows that their position is important. Michelangelo painted the Sistine Chapel by lying on his back. Jazz musicians are supposed to hold their saxophones high and blow confidently through the mouthpiece, filling their lungs with air. The orientiation, position, or posture that you take can help catalyze your creativity. If you normally work at a desk, switch it up. Brainstorm while going for a walk, maybe lie upside down on the ground and stare at the ceiling. Putting your form in different positions can alter the sensations your body feels when interact-ing with the environment, which can trigger creativity!

45

RANDOM TARGET MARKET

In your mind, create the rarest or most unexpected target market you can imagine. You can do this by picking three characteristics of unrelated cultures and combining them to form another culture. Fore example, let's invent a culture that enjoys fire-breathing, spicy foods, and rollercoasters. Based on these three things, you already have enough fuel to start coming up with some creative products that this culture would surely appreciate! Then, you can adapt the product to appeal to a wider audience.

46

MOOD & MUSIC

Certain studies have shown that children who listen to classical music when they're young tend to be more creative when they're older. Regardless of whether you're into Mozart or not, we can get so much inspiration by filling our ears with interesting stimuli. Fill your life with different sounds -- browse new playlists on Spotify; turn on bird/nature sounds in your room; study outside in crowded spaces.

47

HISTORICAL EVENTS

Choose a random date in history, and look the date up on Google. Chances are, some cool events happened that day. Many of those events may have had some sort of problem or conflict that resulted in a solution that commemorates that day. Peruse these events and see if you can come up with other creative solutions to solve those original problems.

48

SIMPLE MACHINE MODELING

They say that all complicated devices are really just made from simple machines. As a refresher, they are: the lever, pulley, wheel & axle, inclined plane, wedge, and screw. Pick a common, but relatively complicated task (such as making eggs in the morning), and design a Rube Goldberg machine using only these simple machines. Then consolidate the entire system into a few simple components, or even better, just one product!

49

SOLVING SHAKESPEARE

So many of Shakespeare's tragedies could have been avoided had the characters had access to technology and a few well designed products. Romeo and Juliet both died due to a simple miscommunication. If only they had downloaded Snapchat. All jokes aside, Shakespeare's plays and other tragedies often have plot holes that could be solved by a simple gadget or invention. Explore these different plot holes as sources of creative inspiration, and you'll enjoy becoming a Shakespeare expert at the same time!

50

PURPOSEFUL POINTLESSNESS

Setting aside time for yourself to relax is essential to recharge and rejuvenate your creative energy. That being said, having a level of intention about the way you replenish your spirit can yield productive results. During "purposeful pointlessness time," you can still relax, but do so in environments that could provide unexpected inspiration. You can wander around hardware stores, or explore new buildings, resting your mind while keeping your eyes and ears active.